The Rainbow Series o
To Touch The

RAINBOW PROMISE

Rainbow Promise

Book Five

Poetry by Chrissy Greenslade.
Illustrations by Jenny Williams.

PETRA PUBLISHING

RAINBOW PROMISE

Copyright © Chrissy Greenslade. 2003

ISBN: 0-9534319-4-0

First Edition published Autumn 2003 by
PETRA PUBLISHING
4, Leven Close
Bournemouth
BH4 9LP

" I dedicate this book to my dear friends,
Pammy & Sadie, Michele, Rosemary, Gilly, Doris, Jill and Joan,
all my beloved friends in 'The Bees',
and to all Friends everywhere. "

Also by Chrissy Greenslade:
Book One - Rainbow of Life
Book Two - Rainbow of The Heart
Book Three - Rainbow of Love
Book Four - Rainbow Magic

British Library Cataloguing in Publication Data:
A catalogue record for this book is available from the British Library

Printed in China through World Print Ltd.

Layout & Design Mark A Fudge
design@fudgie.co.uk / www.fudgie.co.uk

CONTENTS

ACKNOWLEDGEMENTS

The following poems of mine have previously been published in the following magazines and annuals.

Secrets
The Blackbird
First Love

My Weekly
What's it all About?
The Whistler

Peoples Friend
Secrets of The Norfolk Broads
Place of Peace

Chrissy Greenslade thanks all her readers,
who sent such wonderful letters.
If you wish to be informed of forthcoming books in
the Rainbow Series and Stockists please contact:

Petra Publishing,
4, Leven Close,
Bournemouth,
BH4 9LP

Telephone: 01202 762730

E-mail: chrissy@petrapublishing.co.uk   www.petrapublishing.co.uk

INTRODUCTION

After going through one of the most testing periods of my life, I bring you my fifth book in 'The Rainbow Series', 'Rainbow Promise'.

Once again, I bring you hope, comfort, encouragement and laughter. My poems come direct from my heart to yours.

Last year was extremely busy and exciting with Book Signings, Poetry Readings and Craft and Gift Fairs. These were a great success. Also, Jonathan Horrocks, a brilliant, American composer, came to visit me in the summer. We are hoping to work together on compositions in the future. He has already set three of my poems to music (written for singers and an orchestra).

Thank you for writing to tell me that my books are being read at your church gatherings, meetings, at social afternoons and concerts & poetry groups etc. This is wonderful! A reader also told me, that my books have affected, for the better, the lives of every member of her family in some way. Her father had discovered my books and bought them for her each birthday, which filled her with joy. She said that it had brought her father and her closer together because she hadn't realised he appreciated her love of poetry. Also her two children used my books for a project on poetry and have received acclaim for their work from their school. Recently, she sent a copy of my poem 'The Dress Fitting' from Rainbow of Life to her sister, for her daughter's wedding. She and her sister had not been on speaking terms for months. This healed the rift! That is what my Rainbow Books are all about! Bringing joy and peace into your life.

This year has been my testing time. I held onto my Rainbow's promise during the traumatic time of my beloved husband's illness with Motor Neurone Disease, until his passing on May 18th. More than ever now, I believe in my Rainbow and the strength that God gives me, knowing that my Cliff lives on, whole and well again.

A friend recently said to me 'How awful to have lost two husbands'. I replied 'Oh no! How blessed I have been to have had two wonderful marriages'. So many don't even have one!

Look for your blessing each day. Turn to your strength within. Never give up hope. Spread love, kindness and smiles and they will be returned to you. Let us face the future with courage. I hold out my hand of friendship to you. Take it and once again cross over the rainbow with me.

Love and Light, Chrissy

For further information, book requirements, poetry readings and talks please contact
Chrissy Greenslade, Petra Publishing, 4 Leven Close, Bournemouth BH4 9LP
Tel: 01202 762730   E-mail address: chrissy@petrapublishing.co.uk
Internet website address: http://www.petrapublishing.co.uk

THE BLACKBIRD

As I looked out this morning,
Everywhere was drear and still,
The day was slowly waking,
Dewy mist upon the hill.

I sighed at winter's greyness,
At the lateness of the spring,
When suddenly I saw him,
And my heart began to sing.

I smiled at his behaviour,
As he proudly raced around,
His antics were so joyful,
As he hopped across the ground.

His beak was crammed with dry twigs
As he hunted busily,
'I can't waste time' he seemed to say,
As bright-eyed he looked at me

He cocked his head then flew off,
His glad message loud and clear,
'Winter has gone, see for yourself,
That the spring is really here.'

I noticed then a primrose,
And a violet's dainty head,
The mist had gone like my blackbird,
For the wintertime had fled.

THE PERFECT EXAMPLE

'Oh, why do inlaws have to be so perfect and so able?'
I thought as spotless cloth she placed on highly polished table.
The cake she'd made was just the kind shown in a magazine,
It hadn't cracked or sagged a bit as my cake would have been.

Her kitchen neat and tidy, every spoon had its own place,
So streamlined with its gadgets, made my kitchen a disgrace.
Her marmalade was home-made, the fruit scones and biscuits too,
I wish there'd been one brand name or at least a fault or two.

I couldn't find a cobweb and her books were placed so neat,
If she was in our lounge tonight they'd lie around her feet.
Why can't I be domestic, find some joy in dull housework?
The moment that my writing calls I let the spiders lurk.

How can I vac. when golden sunshine's pouring through the door?
Surely for walks, sunbathing is what sunny days are for?
I'll make some cakes tomorrow - I should clean the back window,
I can't do it today because I have the lawn to mow.

Oh dear it's started raining I'll repot this Busy Lizzy,
On second thoughts, I'd better write, tomorrow I'll be busy!

THE STRENGTH OF SILENCE

There isn't a step that is taken,
When God doesn't know where we tread;
For there isn't a word that is spoken
That's unknown to Him as it is said.

He knows what we think how we struggle,
Surrounds us with help when we're weak,
It's enough to acknowledge His presence,
In your quiet surrender- don't speak.

As prayer in your heart lifts in silence,
Tranquillity comes stealing through;
Golden warmth, light and joy, fill your spirit,
As God's power and strength flow in you.

SPRING MADNESS

I've had a sorting, washing session,
I'm on a purge my clothes to freshen,
I've straightened skirts and socks and undies,
I've rehung dresses worn on Sundays.

The clothes I haven't used for ages,
Would fill at least eleven pages,
I've filled the basket full of things,
That's what a sorting session brings.

My folded nighties will need ironing,
The massive pile I'm undermining,
There's no more room to hang the clothes,
My woollies, blouses, hang in rows.

My husband laughs, my arms are aching,
The lines are full, what an undertaking!
Because at the first hint of spring,
He knows that I'll wash everything!

A FRIEND IN NEED

You were there when I cried on your shoulder,
You were there on the day that he died,
And I knew that you saw through the efforts,
My distress and my sadness to hide.

It was you the dear one I could turn to,
The kind angel who kept me supplied
With my soap, underwear and upliftment,
Who was strong and stood by when I cried.

You dear friend held my hand, saw the suffering,
Which tore my darling husband in two,
When you took on your shoulders my problems,
Dearest friend what an angel were you.

You took over financial arrangements,
And helped me to begin my new life,
As we clung to each other consoling,
The fact life had been slashed with a knife.

Only recently you'd lost your loved one,
How you'd cried then when I held your hand,
And I shared all your sorrow, your heartbreak,
So I knew that you could understand.

I shall never forget all your kindness,
You were there when I faced my worst test,
Oh my dear, only God can repay you,
For my friend you are one of the best.

BAD HABITS

We eat far too much of the bad things,
And never enough of the good,
We sit much too long at computers,
Do not exercise knowing we should.

We all of us watch too much TV,
Don't stroll in the country enough,
We eat rubbish foods, peanuts, chocolates,
Get depressed watching News and such stuff.

We travel on buses but don't walk,
When we know that it's really not far,
We hurry and rush don't allow time,
It's much quicker if we go by car.

We're trying to change our bad habits,
Attempting to eat healthy things,
I'm getting up now an hour earlier,
So enjoying the freedom that brings.

We're going for our daily walk now,
Though it usually ends at the shops,
But as this puts a limit on carrying,
Over spending it certainly stops.

We're glowing with pride and with virtue,
But now it is pouring with rain,
The chocolates, T.V. are enticing,
So we're into bad habits again!

WHAT'S IT ALL ABOUT?

"Oh, Christmas is for children", parents say and nod their heads,
"Such stress for us until they're safely tucked into their beds.
Our money wasted, over-spent on toys that will be broken,
It's getting worried, over-tired, bad-tempered words are spoken.

Time writing cards when post is dear, big efforts letter-writing,
The joy of putting up the tree so often ends in fighting.
There's turkey basting, trifle making, parcels still unwrapped,
So much to do and think about, our energy is sapped."

But when we sit around the fire on Christmas afternoon,
We feel so peaceful, satisfied, time passes all too soon.
How lovely is the music of the children's happy cries,
Their efforts with our Christmas gifts bring tears into our eyes.

We know it's all tradition that we eat and drink too much,
But every laugh of pleasure every childish, loving touch,
Stays tucked inside a little glowing corner of our heart,
And gives the New Year coming in, a happy, hopeful start.

'SCOFFALOT'

My husband won't believe it
That I never enjoyed food,
In fact he laughs and says some things,
Which are distinctly rude.

Well it was true at twenty-two,
When I weighed seven stone,
"You eat just like a little bird",
My mom and dad would moan.

He says "You eat much more than me,
You eat just like a horse,
And you are on your pudding when
I'm still on my first course."

To diet sheets I must admit,
I don't pay much attention,
That I really enjoy my food.
I'm not ashamed to mention.

I love my cakes all creamy and
Chocolates, roast meals, the lot,
So laughingly I now confess,
I'm just a 'Scoffalot!

THE VIXEN

She stealthily climbed down the steps,
Her padded feet uttered no sound,
Her nostrils traced the source of food,
As hungrily she searched the ground.

Her body thin, coat drab and dull,
Her ears alert, eyes full of fear,
She ate until her mouth was full,
Her sharp eyes knowing all was clear.

She took morsels away with her,
To some secure and hidden lair,
Then fervently as I observed,
I sent for her a loving prayer,

That foxes would be chased no more,
By men and hounds to give them sport,
That mankind would let love replace,
Such cruelty with their support.

Each day I fed her and she looked,
Now plump, her coat, a silky sheen,
And then today to my delight,
There are now three, where one had been.

Two baby cubs, so sweet she's brought,
Quite unafraid but watchful still,
She stands aside, watches them play,
Now they have drunk and ate their fill.

So on the wings of prayer I ask,
No man will make them suffer pain,
For love will win then gradually,
Mankind and fox can trust again.

NOT SO WET

Women can be thought weak creatures,
They're emotional and cry,
Can't stand a mouse and scream and shout,
If a spider passes by.

But a female's like a teabag
When she's calm, not in a tizz,
As when she's in hot water she
Then will show how strong she is!

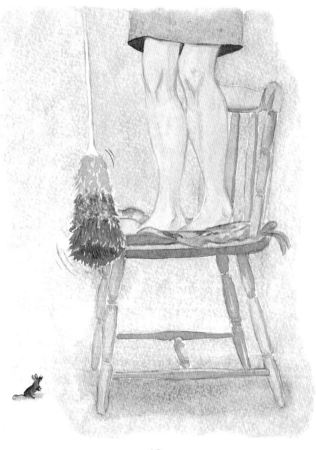

GIVE THEM RELIEF

Whatever the issue, wherever the war,
A problem is there that we cannot ignore,
If countries are laden with billions they owe,
There's nowhere, just nowhere their earnings can go;

Except on the interest and basics to live,
With nothing left over for self-help to give.
We know some dictators bought arms not new hope,
Left helpless, starved people to struggle and cope.

But leaders intending to progress, do good,
With such crippling debts cannot do as they should.
We all have free choice but it's not what God planned,
The fate of these countries to hold in our hand.

To stand by and watch as lands dwindle and fade,
Because of the debt we insist should be paid;
To watch countries suffer, disintegrate, die,
Is something outrageous- we can't shut an eye.

For we are responsible, we have much more,
Now we can show mercy, what 'brothers' are for.
It seems we've forgotten, whatever our creed,
That we are one family, theirs is our need.

A need to be loved, to at least be well fed,
To make life more equal not butter our bread.
We know there must be a progressive release,
To make sure malpractice and fighting will cease.

But let's start with countries who try to succeed,
Who struggle to progress in spite of their need,
So say they don't have to pay back, set them free,
And help the third world find its true liberty.

WATCH OUT, CHRISSY'S ABOUT!

It is no good to ask when will words start to rhyme
For a poem can come anywhere, anytime,
In a café, the street, in the car or in town,
Words will simply slip in which I have to write down.

I can wake from my sleep with a line on my lips,
And a poem can flow between my coffee sips,
Just a hint or a joke, a sad tale or a scene,
Will then inspire words where emotion has been.

So be careful, beware if you spend time with me,
As the source of a poem, my friend you could be,
For on newspaper edges I'll write down a verse,
And if it is today's and not read yet, what's worse?

For my nearest and dearest is often the source
Of my poems, - yet still doesn't want a divorce!
And believe it or not but it really is true,
That my last masterpiece came to life in the loo!

But I am very glad that God gave me this gift,
And I hope that my poetry brings your life a lift,
But beware if I catch you when you look a sight,
For you'll surely be in the next poem I write!

FREEDOM

I'm free as a bird
In my deep meditation,
My soul has been filled
With such joy and elation.

Where sadness and turmoil
My faith has been testing,
In calm contemplation,
My mind has been resting.

I feel that my burden
Now God is removing,
This hushed hour alone is
God-sent I've been proving.

My life filled with pressure,
And thoughts in a riot,
My healing took place,
Thank you God, in the quiet.

A LADY'S HANDBAG

They come in every size and shape,
Their colours every hue,
And what we carry 'round with us,
Men can't believe is true.

The weight can be incredible,
So heavy, you would think,
That everything was tucked inside,
Except the kitchen sink.

Our housekeys, make up, wallet, purse,
Hairbrush, pen, mobile phone,
Umbrella, notebook, glasses, sweets
Cause our loved ones to moan.

"Why ever do you carry all
This clutter everywhere?
You'll never need half of these things!"
But Ladies, do we care?

I'd rather have a torchlight,
And we often need small change,
Though I confess coins weigh a ton,
Some things I'll rearrange.

My bulging bag brings comfort,
And its weight security,
A pity that my right shoulder's
Lopsided, I agree.

I'll do something about it,
Yes dear I do understand,
Look, I have transferred my handbag,
From my shoulder to my hand!

KEEP SEARCHING

When you have been hurt and the sky turns black,
And you're sad and lost with the love you lack,
You must seek within for the reason why,
A person or act has made you cry.

When someone hurts you it's a cry of pain,
Of unhappiness and there is no gain
In reacting badly, so just forgive,
And this will affect the way you live.

As you understand and new strength streams through,
Tolerance will change all the things you do,
And the thoughts you had which depressed you so,
You will find have gone and you will know

That all things will change, there's another day,
It's a further lesson on your pathway,
And the fact you've turned to strength within,
Has relieved, transformed the state you're in.

With a new insight hope begins to stir,
You will face things that in the day occur,
With a shrug, detachment, disperse despair,
For relief and calm are waiting there.

As you accept now what has gone, what's been,
You are feeling better, your thoughts serene,
Hold your head up high, your new life begin,
For composed you'll find that love will win.

FACE LIFT

As the years creep along undetected,
We forget how we laughed at old age,
Never dreaming how close it was coming,
As each birthday displayed a new page.

But because we know youth is inside us,
It's the eternal you that is real,
We agree that old age is a label,
And we're all just as old as we feel.

For there's no such disease known as old age,
And so many grow younger it seems,
In retirement we start to enjoy life,
And begin to bring true all those dreams.

Now with freedom and hobbies for pleasure,
Whether single or still a housewife,
It's delightful to know at the moment,
We can choose what we do with our life.

Still we all envy those with a face lift,
Which can prove that they really are young,
For each morning we look in the mirror,
Puzzled from where those wrinkles have sprung!

But we all can have our 'home-made' face-lift,
Which works great, well it still does with me,
Now at six as I look in the mirror,
The 'before' look declares I'm sixty.

But my 'after' face beams with elation,
As transformed new hope wings me to heaven,
What has happened? I've put on my make-up,
Which I wasn't then wearing at seven.

NOVEMBER SEASCAPE

The sun broke through the gathering clouds,
A silver path traced on the sea,
As grey waves tossed their foamy heads,
Gulls screamed and quarrelled greedily.
A tinge of pink now filled the sky,
As light spread over hazy coasts,
Late promenaders with their dog,
Watched bobbing buoys and distant boats.

From heavenly realms the rays shone down,
Painting skyscapes with glistening gold,
A brave lone bather coasted waves,
Oblivious of the damp and cold.
As waves now lashed the break-water,
And splashed their spray and roared their power,
I sat and thanked God for the peace,
And beauty of this precious hour.

WINTER HOLIDAY

I flicked at the flies as he stifled his sighs,
As the cloud won its race with the sun,
We had tried once again, on this island off Spain,
To wallow in warmth and in fun.

In Spain, the Canaries, so rarely had rain,
That our doubts we'd again cast aside.
But as waves roared and rattled and rain storms we battled,
We could have yelled murder or cried.

It wasn't the villa but weather the killer,
No! The shrubs, swimming pool were all charming,
And it wasn't the food, the surroundings, the mood,
But contrast in heat, so alarming.

We'd thought that it might be a bit cold at night,
But this cold and rainfall wasn't on!
We would never have guessed that we'd both need a vest,
Or odds on we'd never have gone.

Three times we have tried so now we can decide
Just exactly what we're going to do,
Though in England we know there is probably snow,
Winter holidays make us feel blue.

We're going to refrain now from going to Spain,
To our old haunts soon we will return,
In late spring we've agreed, when the sun's guaranteed,
We'll go where the sun doesn't burn.

For in Fuerteventura, there's nothing can lure 'yer',
When you're tossed from hot weather to ice,
Maybe I've over-stressed it, you'll never have guessed it,
They won't catch us going there twice!

SHARED HEALING

We'll send our love and healing
To friends where'er they are,
No matter if they're close to us,
No matter near or far.

A thought has wings, will reach them,
Love's healing still astounds,
And when it's channelled from the Source,
Then healing knows no bounds.

We don't need time to send thoughts,
It takes only a minute,
And think of all the good it does,
When we share together in it.

THE CHALET

A beach chalet, we'd hire, we decided,
So that we could spend days by the sea,
And we wouldn't be selfish we'd share it,
With our friends and with our family.

Oh a fortnight! How great was the first day,
We took games, books and lots of nick-nacks,
And a picnic, binoculars, umbrella -
It's amazing how much that one packs.

Now the chalet it was quite expensive,
It was worth it, we said heartily,
But we found that when we approached 'Eden',
It cost fortunes to park by the sea.

Just for once we said we wouldn't worry,
As outside we both settled but found,
That we needed warm clothes and a blanket,
For a keen wind was whipping around.

So inside with crosswords we retreated,
With our books and a hot cup of tea,
But the wasps were a pest we decided,
As one settled on my hubby's knee.

Foaming froth on the waves was entrancing,
As we filled up our lungs with salt-air,
For at least out of season was peaceful,
We both smiled a relaxed, chalet pair.

Oh, no! Pattering chattering, children,
With their mother and father – Oh help!
We both winced – bringing Hi Fi, no earphones –
There was worse! We then heard a dog yelp.

The next day when it rained, we felt guilty,
We had paid for it, oh what a waste!
To be home, was so nice, back to normal,
In our hearts now the truth we both faced.

The next time we enjoyed a beach picnic,
With our friends who came just for the day,
How they loved it – but they weren't committed,
We were sighing as we packed away.

For we'd have to get up in the morning,
As the forecast was settled and sunny,
Obliged, as we felt we must use it,
It was really so daft and not funny

We would love it next day, we determined,
Though it was much too cold for a swim,
But then neither of us would admit that
A beach chalet to rent was a whim.

But we did make the best of our two weeks,
We relaxed, playing cards or a game,
Fancy missing our routines and hobbies,
Even chores! Our lives just weren't the same.

The last day as we packed up our nick-nacks,
Such exciting thoughts came to a head,
Of things waiting at home that we could do,
And the next day? A morning in bed!

THE FUNNY SIDE

There's a funny situation,
In most everything you do,
Whether you will think it's funny,
Really does depend on you.

Now for instance just this morning,
Something did come to a head,
My alarm went off unheeded,
So I was late out of bed.

With so much to do, I hurried,
Showered then rolled up my hair,
When I tried to wear my sweater,
I was soon in dire despair.

For I realised I should have dressed
Then put my rollers in,
For the problem I was facing,
Caused frustration to begin.

I had thought that I'd just manage,
To pull clothes over my head,
But too late I knew I should have
Used a cardigan instead.

I was feeling claustrophobic,
And I thought I'd faint away
Then I heard a burst of laughter,
Oh this really made my day!

For my other half had woken,
He had seen my sorry plight,
But to see the funny side then
Was too hard, try as I might.

I tugged at the sweater blindly,
Then I tripped, fell on the bed,
As he laughed he came to help me,
Just imagine what I said!

But next time I'll not be stupid,
Wear a neck not quite so tight,
And of course it was quite funny,
Well at least now in hindsight!

ETERNITY

"Eternity, what does this mean?" a friend asked,
"It's so vague, it's not clear, it's unreal;
What's it like, where is it, it's completely unknown,
When I'm there, will I see, hear or feel?"

"It's not in the future, it's now", I replied,
For your soul holds your future today,
It is how you respond, how you feel deep inside,
It's revealed in the words that you say.

With kindly reactions and each loving thought,
Soon Eternity comes into sight,
For as you live with God there's no future to fear,
For you're paving the way with your light.

Eternity's now and the future is now,
And the past was a lesson to learn,
Just accept each event, for the reason they're sent,
And you'll always know which way to turn.

We're told it's the state of the time after death,
But that time's but a link in the chain,
It is now and forever, which nothing can sever,
Live with God and you'll live life again."

THE CAMELLIA

The camellia rejoiced in the warmth of the sun,
As it sleepily plumped up its bud,
For it wasn't aware it was still winter time,
That the weather sometimes wasn't good.
Other plants, bulbs and flowers still slept till the spring,
Waiting for the right time they should wake,
For the seasons were there to provide them with rest,
So that they had less efforts to make.

The camellia swelled then it burst into bloom,
Now a picture in crimson and green,
And it flirted and tossed its bright head in the breeze,
Full of beauty, not cold but serene.
Then one grey winter morning it felt something soft,
Cold, yet warm was its cover of white,
As a blanket of snow draped around like a cape,
What a glorious, delicate sight.

When it bowed its flower heads, it was not in despair,
But paid tribute to winter's kind thought,
For to keep it so warm, till the sun brought a thaw,
Was the care my camellia sought.
So it nestled and slept in its blanket of snow,
Till the sun soothed and washed it at noon,
And then drying its petals and leaves in the warmth,
It bloomed bravely for spring would come soon.

TAKE TIME

Now I know that they say it is lucky,
When you put on your clothes inside out,
But I know I will feel pretty silly,
If I don't change when friends are about.

If I'm late and I really must hurry,
To catch buses or go to the shop,
Oh how often I've fastened my buttons,
Just to find I've missed one at the top.

I've discovered some tights have a habit,
Of deciding which leg feels quite right,
And unless I remove and replace them,
They'll feel twisted from morning till night.

There are bed-socks so fluffy and cosy,
Which when new are a perfect delight,
But once worn they get lost in the bedclothes,
And my feet are ice-cold in the night.

Now to tie up my shoes is an effort,
In a hurry a shoelace can break,
And this pair are the shoes that are needed,
And there isn't a spare lace to take.

How annoying are these irritations,
Much more care I will take, just you see,
I'll allow lots of time to get ready,
Then these things will not happen to me.

SILENT WORSHIP

There's a beautiful feeling of stillness,
There's a hush and the coo of a dove,
There is harmony, union and healing,
As my silence is filling with love.

There's a light that is waiting and shining,
To reach into the core of my heart,
There's a longing, a yearning for contact,
Where direction and guidance will start.

As I bathe in this beautiful oneness,
With the flame of God's light burning bright,
The true meaning of life's way and purpose,
Very soon will be brought into sight.

So I'll rest and let go of my worries,
I'll link in with the strength of the Word,
For I know I can be very certain,
That the thoughts that I think will be heard.

SUCCESS

I saved up for a video,
It was my fervent dream
To tape those oldies, black and white,
Which are so evergreen.

I watched then with excitement,
As it was tried and set,
But as instructions were explained,
I knew I would forget.

As I was left bewildered,
Facts swimming in my head,
My shaken confidence returned,
The Manual I re-read.

I could record a picture,
The one that now I saw,
But my attempts to pre-record,
Were flickers, nothing more.

I phoned the shop assistant,
My husband shook his head,
For electronics weren't his scene,
He looked on them with dread.

I was obsessed and frantic,
Frustration knew no end,
But once I'd mastered all the steps,
He knew I'd be his friend.

Just wait until that good film,
Which is too late at night
Is taped by me, then he can see
It when the time is right.

I've tried so long I don't care,
Determinedly I press
The buttons … Joy! I've got it right!
Yippee! At last success!

THE NEW HAIR-STYLE

I thought I'd have my hair restyled,
A new image I desired,
I looked at glossy magazines,
I enthused and felt inspired.

They snipped and curled and combed and crimped,
Till transformed I went my way,
But as my husband passed me by,
Now I wondered what he'd say.

"Good heavens, it's you! What have they done?"
His poor face it looked quite white,
I felt upset until I saw
My reflection – he was right!

"Don't worry dear, I'll brush it through,
I just thought I'd like a change,
It really will not take me long,
This new style to rearrange.

Exotic curls soon disappeared,
As relieved my hubby smiled,
"Oh that is great. It does look nice,
Now by you it's been restyled!"

I REMEMBER

What I remember from years long ago,
In war time we slept in the room down below.
"Quick, get the children safe under the bed",
Shouted my father and my mother said:

"Under the bed now quick under the bed".
We scrambled so quickly that I bumped my head.
We weren't afraid as we giggled and pushed,
Only poor mother was worried and rushed.

Donald my brother was in mother's arms,
He slept through the noise and the siren alarms.
Not enough room for my brother and us,
Under the bed with such haste and such fuss.

Bombers flew deadly and droned overhead,
They threatened all those who weren't under the bed,
We knew what to do at the sound of dad's voice,
Had to behave for dad gave us no choice.

War songs we sang like 'The White Cliffs of Dover',
The enemy planes with their buzz bombs flew over,
'Run Rabbit Run', as we sat hand in hand,
We children sang as they threatened our land.

But our brave dad, who worked shifts, stayed in bed,
While bombers zum-zummed in the dark overhead.
Wouldn't close his eyes till he heard the 'All Clear'.
Knew skies were empty of bloodshed and fear.

Giggling we sang as our mum nearly wept,
We quarrelled and teased whilst my brother still slept.
Silence was heard, such a frightening one,
Bombs whistling past as the damage was done.

Bombs passed us over – hit factories instead,
Our dad and the 'All Clear' sent us back to bed.
I'll never forget those eight words my dad said,
So long ago in the room overhead.

SLOW DOWN TO A GALLOP

I ate a hasty breakfast,
I rushed to sweep the floor,
I quickly did the washing,
With speed I closed the door.

I dashed to post a letter,
I raced to catch the bus,
Was late for my appointment,
Which caused a lot of fuss.

I try to do things quickly,
So I'll not fret and worry,
But the results are just the same,
I'm always in a hurry.

THOUGHTS OF HOME

Why is it when a week has passed,
And I am far away,
I find a corner of my heart,
Begins to ache each day?
It's really almost physical,
A little yearning pain,
A longing for our well-loved home,
To be there once again.

The peacefulness and quiet of
The lane, the moor, the sea,
The blackberries are forming now,
Tomatoes for our tea.
Ripe apples must be dropping and
The pears grown big and lush,
The gulls and lapwings piercing cries
Disturbing all the hush.

The hedges and our lawns will now
Have grown, be lush and green,
And pyracantha berries where
White flowers would have been.
The roses will be blooming still,
Geraniums vivid red,
And marigolds and tagetes,
Aflame in flower bed.

Our hidden garden chalet tucked
Away from other's view,
Our terrace for sunbathing,
Garden chairs and barbeque;
Neglected, waiting to be used,
For lazing in the sun,
A secret place to contemplate,
As well as having fun.

My writing and my painting,
All the books we love to share,
Are asking for our return home,
So cosy waiting there,
Whatever weather's offered us,
As we come home once more,
The sunshine of its warmth and love,
Extends from door to door.

I clutch your hand, we're home at last,
Content at peace again,
For we are in our haven where
God grant, we can remain.
I smile at all our comfort,
At our lovely, tranquil view,
But most of all because this home
Is filled with love and you.

A MESSAGE FOR YOU

I know I have to write this poem,
Especially for you,
Because there is a message here,
Wondrous, astounding, true.
For life goes on, you cannot die,
You pass to the other side,
And when you leave, the physical you,
Will be the part that died.

For we are pure spirit still,
Inside our bodies now,
And what we can remember
Is the part God will allow.
For we are here for lessons which
Somehow we failed before,
And anyone on earth we meet,
Can open up a door –

To inner truth and insight,
To the light that is within,
And in the meeting of two souls,
Attunement can begin.
I know that you must find your truth,
As everyone should seek,
But if you think life ends on earth,
The future's blank and bleak.

But knowing that the spirit you,
Linked by its golden thread,
When severed at the passing point,
Is vibrant, free, not dead,
Is wonderful, a glowing thought,
The truth that life goes on,
Our spirit body, ether made,
Still there when 'man' has gone.

Your body's like an overcoat,
Which you will cast aside,
And when you meet your loved ones then,
You'll know you haven't died.
In your new life you will progress,
In every stage and plane,
But you can progress quicker when
You know you'll live again.

For if you reach the 'Summerlands',
Deciding it's not real,
You'll not believe you died at all,
And you'll need time to heal.
But keeping your mind open to
The truth you will be told,
You'll find you can look forward and
Not back as you grow old.

You'll find the true meaning of life,
Your doubts and fears decrease,
And answers to your questions will
Surround your soul with peace.
So in the stillness, listen now,
Ask God to hear your plea,
To help you know that we live on,
Be certain, just like me.

Ask God! Don't give up, be sincere,
Let Him resolve your quest,
Just wait, expect an answer and
Then God will do the rest.

GOOD INTENTIONS

Still young I was impulsive for I had not long been wed,
So keen to be a good wife bright ideas buzzed in my head,
I really longed to show him just how much I loved and cared,
But if I'd known the outcome all my thoughts I would have shared.

For when I hung his shirt up and I saw such disarray,
His shoes all muddled, scattered, I thought that I'd make his day.
I tidied up his footwear standing his shoes on parade,
But starting on his clothing was the mistake that I made.

I put his suits and jackets and his jerseys, waistcoats, shirts,
Each on a separate hanger but this is the part that hurts –
I spent ages untying all the knots left in his ties,
And as I hung his trousers up, I even zipped the flies.

Not four things on one hanger, now each cardigan was folded,
It looked so organised how could I know that I'd be scolded?
When he returned at tea-time, how on earth was I to know,
That he had loved them as they were? He could have told me so.

"Chrissy, why did you do this, oh it really isn't fair,
I'd sorted them to make it quick, I don't have time to spare;
I'd grouped them all together and the colours mixed and matched,
I knew exactly what to wear, ties ready and attached.

Oh no you haven't Chrissy! You have untied all my ties!"
His voice was raised, I trembled, as despair shone in his eyes.
"When I'm late it's so easy pulling them over my head,
Well now they'll all need ironing". No more needed to be said.

By now my tears were flowing. "Oh I thought that you'd be glad,
That all my work would please you, not upset you, make you sad."
My loved one soon forgave me for so good was my intention,
But from that time my bright ideas I was always sure to mention.

OPTIMISM

I'm looking on the bright side for today I know I'll cope.
For positive's my pass-word, I feel well and filled with hope.
My lethargy is passing and later I'll have a rest,
And I'll make sure my garden tasks are ones I like the best.

For months I've planned to do this, it's hard work I must confess,
But oh what satisfaction when I've cleared up all the mess
That's cluttering up the garage, there's so much to throw away,
Then maybe I can have a walk, it's such a lovely day.

Oh dear it's started raining, I'm resigned, I'll stay inside,
For in the garage I'll have air, the door is open wide.
I've cleared out lots of rubbish, have an overflowing bin,
But nothing is a problem when this positive state I'm in.

The phone is ringing but I'm sure whoever speaks to me,
Will get the right reception 'cause of my positivity.
My day's been full and busy, I have kept my spirits high -
Oh No! The bin's blown over and I think I'm going to cry!

THE CHRISTMAS PRESENT

On Christmas Eve in Singapore,
We heard the sound of knocking,
And as my friend then told her tale,
We found her story shocking.

A little puppy in her arms,
At me was sadly gazing,
The fact that it had still survived
Its ordeal was amazing.

It had a paw that wasn't black,
'Bad luck' by Chinese thinking,
Thrown in the monsoon drain to die,
Hopes to survive were sinking.

But whimpers and its yelps of fear,
Were heard by English neighbours,
Who having climbed into the drain,
Were rewarded for their labours.

They brought the little dog to us,
To comfort and to cherish,
For they knew that we wouldn't let
A little puppy perish.

So we gave it a taste of life,
Protected, fed and pampered,
We called the puppy Christmas,
And its presence never hampered.

But one sad day, my little dog,
Now sleek-coated and growing,
Followed me as I left the house
Unaware where he was going.

The end was swift, the car was big,
His precious life a token,
And as my little Christmas died,
I felt my heart was broken.

We hadn't had him very long,
But Christmas was a treasure,
And all the love I felt for him,
I couldn't weigh or measure.

And how we missed that little soul,
His naughty ways, his playing.
I blamed myself for carelessness,
His exit not delaying.

But in his Puppy Heaven,
Where he'll play for evermore,
He wags his tail and waits with joy
For his friends in Singapore.

CLOCK WATCHING.

Today I've stopped clock-watching,
Will be 'laid-back', let things 'be',
Not planning things throughout the day,
Stop being busy me.

I'm finding it not easy,
For I got up much too late,
Then breakfast was at half past ten,
And lunchtime had to wait.

The day is hot and sunny,
So I'll sunbathe, read a book,
I don't know what time's supper or
When I'll work on my book.

The meat is still defrosting
And my chores are well behind,
I haven't listed things to do,
I'm restless in my mind.

I've just seen what the time is,
So I'm going back inside,
I've tidied up the sitting room,
I mustn't let things slide.

There's just time for some writing,
When I've had a cup of tea,
Oh I find it much better,
Being clock-watching busy me!

'BEE' GUIDED

The alphabet's a guide it's true,
Study the A B C,
You'll know which letter is for you,
Of course the letter B.

This really is significant,
It gives the rules divine,
And if you concentrate on them
Your future will be fine.

Be happy, cheerful and bright,
Be helpful, thoughtful kind,
For every B spells out your life,
If you keep it in mind.

Be patient, calm and tolerant,
Behave and do no wrong,
Be likeable and lovable,
Accept what comes along.

Be nice to those who try you most,
Believe in all that's true,
Be generous in every act,
It will come back to you.

Bestow your smile on those around,
Make other people glad,
Be understanding, empathise,
When other folk are sad.

Be a good listener and be wise,
So many B's there are,
But if you study you will know
What kind of 'Bee' you are.

Be gentle and forgiving but
Be strong and be detached,
For even the most hurtful things,
And quarrels can be patched.

For you cannot be unkind or
Be spiteful when you know,
That Bees choose only pure things,
Their product to bestow.

From flowers bees bring healing,
Nourishment, both rich and whole,
So your choice from the alphabet,
Will help you reach your goal.

WEARING WELL

So distinctive the dress, so outrageous the price,
But it isn't the price that can make it look nice.
Yes the cut may be great, oh so chic a la mode,
But you won't cause a stir if you stand pigeon toed.
If your shoulders are hunched or you stand on one leg,
Then you might just as well buy your dress off the peg.

MY ADDRESS BOOK

I turn the pages slowly,
In front of me I see,
A record of the friends and folk,
Whose lives have linked with me.

Our holiday addresses,
Bring memories clear and bright,
A school-friend I would like to trace,
Perhaps this year I'll write.

Names of dear friends departed,
Still bring a loving tear,
For always they are close to me,
This season of the year.

My book is thumbed and tatty,
But each name holds a link,
These people played a little part
In how I live and think.

Although some names are crossed out
On this my Christmas list,
I talk to them and send them love,
In thought they won't be missed.

But I can see this Christmas
My list is still no less,
For now I have lots of new friends,
To share more happiness.

THAT CERTAIN AGE

Whatever is the matter with
Myself and with my moods?
Although I am a cheerful soul,
This other self intrudes.
She gets depressed, her nerves on edge
Sometimes she's lost and sad,
She gets worked up for nothing and
Her changes make me mad.

In fact I am quite happy and
My life is full and good,
But then this other me bursts out,
More often than she should.
I cannot understand her as
She takes this hold on me,
I really do detest her and
Of her I must be free.

Now vitamins and H.R.T.,
On her a battle wage,
And hopefully I'll lose her till
I've passed this 'funny age'.
Soon all will be forgiven as
Repenting in a rush,
I'll get rid of these symptoms and
That threatening hot flush.

The real me now is coping and
Results I am assured,
Are wonderful and soon I'll be,
So gracefully matured.
As like a precious wine that's had
The time to rest and blend,
I'll do the same and know that I
Shall triumph in the end.

Then after fermentation time,
Like wine mellowed and sweet,
You'll know the other me has had
Her day, is in retreat.
So hold on to your patience,
This condition's on the wane,
Soon I shall be my balanced, cheerful,
Normal self again!

DARTMOOR

Strange, mystic stones left stark and still,
Thrones scattered on the moor,
Secretly, standing on a hill,
The silent, silver tor.

What mighty hand has placed you there,
Carved well your shape and face,
Where animals in freedom share
Your kingdom and your grace?

Green-golden ferns now deck
  your side,
With heather, cushion-soft,
The curving lands so far and wide,
A buzzard scans aloft.

Cloud-shadows race, change
  moorland dress,
Each colour pale then bright,
What secret we are left to guess,
Are hidden out of sight.

What kind of man once worked
  this land,
Who toiled and mined for tin?
What elements did they withstand,
What impasse were they in?

We found the source of winding stream,
A fairy glade well hid,
A place where strangers sit and dream,
Where surely they first did.

The answer's hidden in the stones,
If you just care to look,
Expressions show their fears and groans,
Just like a picture book.

They're only piles of stones, you say,
But different is each face,
Some gentle, stark, full of dismay,
Each character you'll trace.

So moorland bathed in soft moonlight,
Guard well your sleeping tor,
For man has hidden out of sight,
The secrets of the moor.

BLIND DATE

At four foot eight, excited,
She thought my dream's come true,
He's handsome, dressy and well off,
And under forty two.

She'd waited for this blind date,
He seemed so very nice,
He picked her up in his sports car,
His after-shave – Old Spice!

His eyes were bright and twinkly,
Manners she could not fault,
She smiled as her heart melted,
Then struck the thunder bolt.

As from the car he clambered,
It wasn't her in heaven,
Because she saw as he stood up,
That he was six foot seven!

ANGEL AMMUNITION

Worries, problems, illness on the earth were everywhere,
The atmosphere so negative, despair was in the air,
With speed the Christmas angels once again prepared their plan,
To bring again peace on the earth, the gift God gave to man.

They saw sad, worried faces all the pressures and the pain,
They watched anxiety appear as Christmas came again,
They flocked into the countries where the war left lame and dying,
And warmed the homeless with their wings and stopped the orphans crying.

The whole time they'd been hoping man would hear the still, small voice,
But knew that mankind always had the power to have free choice.
They couldn't stop their actions but they knew with love and prayer,
They could help man recover and help them to be aware

That silent thought was living and that spoken thought was real,
That through the Word came action, which affects the way we feel.
They knew that what was needed was the love deep in man's heart,
And as the seed began to grow, God's healing power would start.

So in the realms of angels they linked up with those who'd passed,
And thronged the whole world with their love and asked that peace would last,
They turned bad things to good things, put good thoughts into men's heads,
They comforted the lonely and old people in their beds.

They visited each country and each powerhouse, each home,
They sprinkled their love message in each church and mosque and dome,
For though they were unnoticed their peace-work went on unseen,
The changes caused by their great light, shone bright where they had been.

New harmony was spreading as united thoughts now grew,
Upliftment and new hope was born that love would see them through,
For men would live together recognising now his brother,
For the best ammunition is to really love each other.

FIRST LOVE

I met him in the morning,
When grass was full of dew,
And how I blushed bright crimson,
As all my dreams came true.

His eyes were brown and pleading,
My heart filled with delight,
So elegant and charming,
He was a dashing sight.

His head held close to my cheek,
His breath upon my face,
My loving eyes admired him,
His good looks and his grace.

My hand now he was seeking,
He nuzzled it with glee,
I stroked his nose and fed him
- The horse Dad's given me!

THE WHISTLER

He whistles when he's happy,
He whistles when he's sad,
If I've lost him when out shopping,
Of his whistles I am glad.

He whistles Christmas carols,
At Easter and in Lent,
And when in a supermarket,
I can follow where he went.

He drives our neighbours barmy,
Whistling the same old tune,
But I've heard it now for thirty years,
So I really am immune.

But when he's feeling poorly,
Lies silent in his bed
How I wish I'd hear him whistle,
Never mind what others said.

So if your tuneful neighbour,
Warbles his serenade,
Please be tolerant and patient,
For he's healthy I'm afraid!

PLACE OF PEACE

There's a path, there's a hill,
Where the salt-breezes blow,
Tossing damp, tangled locks in my eyes;
Screaming gulls wheel and turn,
Skimming wild seas that churn,
And above me cloud-castled blue skies.

On this path I am free,
My heart filled with content,
Though alone I press on with my dreams;
On the springy-turfed grass,
Rabbits peacefully pass,
Butterflies bask in sparkling sunbeams.

In this magical place,
I shall evermore roam,
It is heaven, a homeland for me;
For my spirit's at rest,
In the place I love best,
And at peace here I ever shall be.

IT'S IN THE BAG

Oh no, where did I put them?
I think I've lost my keys,
They're for the house and for my car,
I've gone weak at the knees.

I search my bag in panic,
But cannot see them there,
Oh why, oh why? I never learn,
I should have keys to spare.

I search inside my handbag,
Unzip the outside pocket,
Imagining the problems loom,
My car, how to unlock it.

There are many compartments,
Some zipped and some unzipped,
I frantically but thoroughly,
Seek where they could have slipped.

Maybe I could have dropped them,
Or left them in my coat,
What shall I do, tell the police?
Fear clutched my heart and throat.

I ransacked then my handbag,
For sections there were five,
But no, here is another one
I'd missed! I made a dive.

Thank God I saw my keys there,
I'll not do this again,
I'll give away this handbag for
It's driving me insane.

There will be no more sections,
In the new bag I buy,
For if I went through this again,
I think that I would die!

THE LOSS OF A CHILD

Oh to lose a child feels you've lost your soul,
You've lost part of you, you're no longer whole,
You feel so much pain, though your tears have dried,
You look calm outside but you weep inside.

And complete families you can still resent,
Why for them such joy, what was God's intent?
And you blame yourself as you blame the world,
As your hurt and anger at friends is hurled.

But the time will come when you're drained and spent,
That you'll understand why this all was meant,
Though you rant and rage it just had to be,
For your tiny child was on loan you see.

As sometimes a child is a special gift,
Sent for a brief time to give you a lift,
A dear angel child who would not survive,
The world pressures if she had stayed alive.

Throughout her sweet life her bright light shone out,
She brought happiness, dispelled sadness, doubt,
And the time she had, though it was so short,
Was exactly right for the things she taught.

Though you can't see her with your physical eye,
She is beautiful for she cannot 'die',
For there is no death only living on,
And she is still there though you think she's gone.

She is just as close as a gentle breath,
She's alive and well for there is no death.
So send her your love, smile and say her name,
For the link you have is still just the same.

Hold her in your heart but let her go free,
Grief will hold her back, tell her you can see,
That you now accept time can heal your pain,
For you know one day you will meet again.

SECRETS OF THE NORFOLK BROADS

The water chuckled 'neath the hull,
As lazily we passed,
And as the windmill came in view,
Its magic spell was cast.

Its sails were still that summer's day,
Hushed, peaceful was the scene,
And all around lay trees and flowers,
So restful and serene.

The cottage dreamed its tranquil dreams,
As wonder took a hold,
But kept its silent secrets well,
Its stories left untold.

Who'd built the cottage and the mill,
Remained a mystery,
We wondered who was living there,
What characters we'd see.

But not a soul we saw who stirred,
On that soft, sleepy day,
We sighed then as, still wondering,
We gazed and sailed away.

RESOLUTION

I'm trying to stay healthy,
I'm giving up sweet things,
I'm finding it not easy,
I've had one of my flings.

As Christmas isn't over,
There are five days before
I must give up the chocolates
And biscuits I adore.

I know it's moderation
That is the correct aim,
But when they're set before me,
My reasons are quite lame.

Today I need some cheering,
Or they will soon go bad,
Each time I find an excuse,
Then later I feel sad.

My waist-band is much tighter,
And blemished is my skin,
But this year's resolution's
To give-up – I shall win.

I know you don't believe it,
And smile in sympathy,
But you'll marvel next summer
When you see the slim-line me!

YOUR GUARDIAN ANGEL

You are never alone for your Angel is near,
Just ask her to come and her voice you will hear.
It won't be aloud but right there in your head,
And you'll smile with relief when you hear what is said.

Now just close your eyes tight, feel God's warmth and His light,
Your Guardian Angel's aware of your plight,
Your worries will vanish as you're wrapped in peace,
As your pains, doubts and worries dissolve and decrease.

You are never alone, your companion is there,
Your own special angel, so never despair,
God sent her for you for He cares, loves you so,
She will uplift and comfort you when you feel low.

So now filled with relief, take new heart, disperse strife,
Strength gained, renewed hope, will refresh, light your life,
Aware that your angel is here on this earth,
Loneliness now will go as you have a rebirth.

Facing life now with courage, your hand she will take,
Walk wisely together for joy is at stake,
How warm is the presence your angel has shown,
Hold your head up - be brave, for you're never alone.

GOD BLESS YOU

From the moment I hear, "May God bless you my dear,"
I know that these words will bring comfort and peace,
For worry and sadness will soon disappear,
As a blessing surrounds you depressions will cease.

For a blessing brings goodness, abundance, a smile,
It sows seeds of healing, relief for a while,
In it lies protection from hurt and from pain,
A renewal of hope given from God once again.

As a blessing is sent from the source of all life,
It's sent as a balm for our suffering, our strife,
A gift that is offered from love that's divine,
It forgives, it supports, it's a comfort, life-line.

So keep sending God's blessings throughout your new day,
To people you meet and to those far away,
Bless tests you are given, you'll find that your sighs,
Really still are God's blessings for you in disguise.

Don't forget you should use these three wonderful words,
Bless friends and bless strangers, bless animals, birds,
Give smiles, take a hand, make your blessings come true,
And you'll find that in life they will come back to you.

'OUT OF THE MOUTHS OF BABES'

How much we learn from children,
 Who will say just what they think,
They make you laugh or get upset,
And can cause your heart to sink.

 When in a supermarket,
 And they start to cry or shout,
 They're only stating what they feel,
 What frustration's all about.

They come out with expressions,
Which can shock, fill you with fear,
For where have you gone wrong
 you think,
But the answer is quite clear.

 They hear things on the T.V.
 From the loud youths in the street,
 You're not to blame when little souls,
 Those same words will repeat.

A child shows it's unhappy,
By loud crying in the night,
How hard for dads and mothers
To decide what's wrong or right.

 Lack of communication,
 For a baby cannot say,
 I'm hungry, hurting, wet or cold,
 So crying is the way.

Children can have a paddy,
Release their tensions, stress,
But when we grown ups hold it back,
We soon find life's a mess.

 So sometimes just like children,
 Our pains we should reveal,
 Say I'm not well, I'm feeling sad,
 Or explain just what we feel.

And when we've aired our grievance,
Like curing a virus bug,
The best and greatest healing is
A loving, heartfelt hug!

RAINBOW PROMISE

Things only can get better
This I can promise you,
Although things seem so hopeless now,
Believe and dreams come true.

In every illness, sadness
Lies compensations, gifts,
And through the cloudy, tear drop days
Your rainbow, life uplifts.

You'll meet a friend to lighten
To brighten up your day,
You'll find a skill, an aim, a word,
To pave with love, life's way.

You'll find that hope's the winner,
It won't declare defeat,
And at your positive approach,
New strength problems will meet.

There'll always be a rainbow
A promise there for you,
For faith and hope, God's loving care
Will help to see you through.

A FEW EXCERPTS FROM READERS LETTERS

"I was given two copies of your books. I couldn't put them down. You cover every occasion and I find them most reassuring and lovely to read. "

Rose Burt , Bournemouth, Dorset.

"My father gave me your delightful books as a birthday present. I was overjoyed . I have four. I am looking for something to hold them together. A ribbon is very nice but perhaps a cover of sorts to hold them to keep them in prime condition. So many of your poems seem meant just for me. I found 'To Dearest Mom' in 'Rainbow of Love' a very special piece. I never knew my Dad cared about my interest in poetry. It has given me a nice feeling to share such special reading with him. Thank you."

Olive Hawkins, Redditch , Worcs.

"This book is another of your miracles of your creation in English literature. A lot of poems from this book are excellent. They are your life and a very strong message for ordinary and special peoples for every government and leadership. They are value for the human minds. I can try to translate this into Albanian."

Petraq Kote, Poet & Secretary of 'Myzeqeta' Cutural and Patriotic Association. Albania

"Your book 'Rainbow Magic is beautifully illustrated and your words are so inspiring. I am absolutely positive that your sincere and beautiful words will inspire countless Crusaders throughout the world."

Brother Andrew, World Healing Crusade, Blackpool. Lancs.

"Not many people put into their poetry what you've put into these poems. Bless you for them."

Elizabeth Meanandadeva, Wells, Somerset.

"Many thanks for your loving books that have just arrived. Your first one of the series is really beautiful and I know that I shall enjoy the new ones as well. You certainly write from the heart. It is a wonderful God-given gift. Good luck in all your writing, dear Chrissy."

Lilian and Andy McCartney, Portsmouth. Hants.

"I have a list of poems from each of your books Chrissy that we would love to put music to. You are a wonderful person, Chrissy so tuned-in it shines from your work. People I've shown your books to- family and friends have been very taken with your poems. Your books say everything. What a gift! You are so open in sharing your innermost feelings, now that's what I call sharing."

Rosemarie Connelly, North Carbrain, Scotland

"Please find enclosed cheque for Book Two and Three. I'm sure I will find them as much a joy as I've found Book One. I have used this book so many times and everyone who hears your poetry loves it. Thank you and God bless you."

Maureen Tew, Crewe, Lancs

"I was given 'The Rainbow of Love' for Christmas from a friend who lives in Dorset. I'm so enjoying it. I think its marvellous! I would so much like the previous two books."

Nora Pas, Kidderminster Worcs

"Many thanks for the fourth book, 'Rainbow Magic' and third book 'Rainbow of Love.' I wish you every success to reach your dream and complete your rainbow."

Love and Peace. Mary Milsom, Warrington, Lancs